The Gospel of Philip

Mystical Teachings on Love, Truth, and the Sacred

A Modern Translation

Adapted for the Contemporary Reader

**Philip the Apostle
(Gnostic Tradition)**

Translated by Tim Zengerink

© **Copyright 2025**
All rights reserved.

It is not legal to reproduce, duplicate, or transmit any part of this document in either electronic means or in printed format. Recording of this publication is strictly prohibited and any storage of this document is not allowed unless with written permission from the publisher except for the use of brief quotations in a book review.

This book contains works of fiction. Any resemblance to persons living or dead, or places, events, or locations is purely coincidental.

Table Of Contents

Preface - Message to the Reader 1

Introduction 5

Gospel of Philip 12

Thank You for Reading 51

Preface - Message to the Reader

What If You Could Help Rebuild the Greatest Library in Human History?

Thousands of years ago, the Library of Alexandria stood as the crown jewel of human achievement — a sanctuary where the collected wisdom of every known civilization was gathered, preserved, and shared freely.

And then, it was lost.

Through fire, conquest, and the slow erosion of time, humanity lost not just books — but ideas, dreams, discoveries, and stories that could have changed the world forever.

Today, the Library of Alexandria lives again — and you are invited to be a part of its restoration.

Our mission is simple yet profound:

To rebuild the greatest library the world has ever known, and to translate all timeless works into every language and dialect, so that no seeker of knowledge is ever left behind again.

By joining our movement to rebuild the modern Library of Alexandria, you become part of an unprecedented mission:

- **Unlimited Access to the Greatest Audiobooks & eBooks Ever Written:**

  Instantly explore thousands of legendary works—Plato, Shakespeare, Jane Austen, Leo Tolstoy, and countless more. All instantly available to read or listen, placing a complete literary universe at your fingertips.

- **Beautiful Paperback & Deluxe Editions at Printing Cost**

  Own any title as an elegant paperback, deluxe hardcover, or stunning collectible boxset—offered to you at true printing cost, delivered straight to your door. Build your personal Library of Alexandria, crafted for beauty, built for durability, and worthy of proud display.

- **Fresh Translations for Modern Readers—in Every Language & Dialect**

  Enjoy timeless masterpieces reimagined in clear, contemporary language—no more outdated phrases or obscure references. Alongside the original versions, we're tirelessly translating these classics into every language and dialect imaginable, ensuring accessibility and understanding across cultures and generations.

- **Join a Global Renaissance of Literature & Knowledge**

    You directly support expanding our library, publishing deluxe editions at true cost, translating works into all global languages, and bringing humanity's greatest stories to people everywhere. By joining today, you're not just preserving a legacy of masterpieces; you set in motion a powerful wave of literary accessibility.

Become a Torchbearer of Knowledge.

Join us for free now at LibraryofAlexandria.com

Together, we will ensure that the light of human wisdom never fades again.

With gratitude and a shared love of knowledge,

The Modern Library of Alexandria Team

Visit:

www.libraryofalexandria.com

Or scan the code below:

Introduction

Love as Revelation: The Gnostic Path to Union

The Gospel of Philip is one of the most profound and poetic texts in the corpus of Gnostic literature. Discovered in the Nag Hammadi Library in 1945 and written in Coptic, this extraordinary work is attributed to Philip the Apostle—not in the sense of authorship, but in the tradition of early Christian mystical authority. It is not a gospel in the narrative style of Matthew or John; it does not recount the life or sayings of Jesus in a linear fashion. Instead, it is a collection of sayings, reflections, metaphors, and spiritual revelations—a sacred tapestry woven from fragments of divine wisdom. This gospel challenges its reader not to learn doctrine, but to awaken to love, light, and the inner path of sacred union.

At its heart, The Gospel of Philip offers a meditation on the nature of divine love and spiritual transformation. It speaks not of commandments and law but of knowledge (gnosis), intimacy, and the deep reconciliation of opposites—heaven and earth, male and female, body and spirit. Its vision of salvation is not one of obedience to external authority, but of inner awakening to the divine image within the soul. Love is the key: not romantic sentiment, but sacred union—the healing of the division that came from ignorance and separation. The gospel presents love as revelation, a force that does not merely feel, but illuminates, penetrates, and transforms. Love is the path to knowing. To love deeply is to perceive truth. To unite in love is to restore what has been broken since the beginning of time.

This text does not speak plainly. It uses paradox, metaphor, and symbolic language to express truths that ordinary language cannot contain. Its vision is mystical and its expressions often elusive, like glimpses of light in a darkened mirror. To read The Gospel of Philip is to enter into mystery—not the mystery of confusion, but of depth. It reveals what can be known only through inward seeing, through the opening of the heart to divine presence. In this way, it follows the path of the mystics and the Gnostics: it does not tell you what to believe—it invites you to see for yourself.

The gospel presents the idea that what is truly sacred is hidden from those who look only with the eyes of the body. Baptism, anointing, the bridal chamber, and resurrection—all are symbols of inner transformation. These are not mere rituals, but thresholds of experience through which the soul passes as it awakens to its true nature. The bridal chamber, in particular, stands as one of the most powerful symbols in the text: a place of sacred union where the soul is joined with its divine counterpart, and where the fragmented self becomes whole. This is not simply about sexual or human love—it is about divine eros, the longing of the soul to return to the source from which it came.

Jesus is not depicted here as a distant savior or moral teacher, but as a revealer of mysteries. He is the one who unveils what has been hidden, who invites the soul into knowledge of itself, and who models the reconciliation of flesh and spirit. His teachings, as presented in this text, are radically intimate. They call each person not to external conformity, but to inward rebirth. The divine light is not somewhere else—it is within. The goal is not escape from the world, but transformation of the self through the recognition of the divine presence already at work.

The Symbolic Language of Truth

The Gospel of Philip is structured not as a single narrative but as a series of sayings and reflections, many of which build upon one another in themes and symbols. To read it is to navigate a labyrinth of meanings. Each passage is a door, and the key is not logic but contemplation. The language of the text is intentionally symbolic, because it speaks of realities that cannot be reduced to literal definitions. The sacred is not confined to words; it lives in the space between them, in the resonance they create in the soul.

Much of the text is built around reinterpretations of traditional Christian sacraments and ideas: baptism, chrism (anointing), the Eucharist, resurrection, and the bridal chamber. But unlike orthodox expressions of Christianity, these are not viewed merely as outward ceremonies—they are seen as inner mysteries. Baptism is not only the washing with water but the immersion into divine knowledge. Chrism is not simply oil on the body but the fragrance of divine presence. The Eucharist is not only bread and wine but the feeding of the inner light. And resurrection is not only something that happens after death, but something the soul must experience now, in this life, by awakening from spiritual sleep.

The text repeatedly emphasizes that what is real and lasting cannot be seen by the eyes of the world. What is born of the flesh perishes, but what is born of spirit endures. Thus, those who are ruled by the senses remain outside the mystery. Only those who seek truth within themselves—those who love the hidden, who trust the heart, who open themselves to silence—can receive what is being offered. The "hiddenness" of God is not a punishment or a trick, but an invitation to go deeper.

Truth must be loved in order to be known.

The gospel's symbolic use of gender also plays a central role. The sacred union of male and female is presented not only as a metaphor for divine reconciliation, but as a way of understanding the soul's journey. Just as Adam and Eve were divided, so the human soul is divided from its spiritual counterpart. Redemption is the rejoining of that which was separated. In this light, the bridal chamber becomes the place of ultimate healing, where the opposites within the soul are reconciled, where alienation ends, and where the human being becomes one again—whole, luminous, and alive in the divine.

Mary Magdalene appears in this text not simply as a historical figure but as a spiritual archetype. She is portrayed as the beloved of Jesus, not in the sense of mere affection, but as the one who understood his teaching most deeply. She is the figure of awakened wisdom, the embodiment of the feminine soul that longs for union with the Logos, the Word. Her presence challenges traditional assumptions and elevates the feminine dimension of divinity and human experience. She is not lesser but luminous, not subordinate but spiritually central. In her, the divine speaks through the voice of love.

This modern translation has been carefully crafted

to preserve the poetic depth and symbolic nuance of the original, while making it accessible to contemporary readers. Every line has been rendered with clarity and reverence, allowing the deeper meanings to emerge gradually, as they were intended. The archaic style of older translations has been gently reshaped to reveal the living spirit beneath the words, without diminishing the mystery. This version is not a commentary—it is a living reflection of the original, offered as a companion for your own spiritual journey.

Awakening the Light Within

To read The Gospel of Philip today is to encounter a voice from the ancient world that speaks with uncanny immediacy to the inner life. It does not seek to convert, to condemn, or to divide—it seeks to awaken. It tells the reader that the divine is not distant, but present within the soul. That truth is not imposed, but revealed in love. That the journey is not outward, but inward. And that salvation is not merely to be forgiven, but to be reunited—to become whole again.

This gospel does not provide simple answers. It provides pathways. It does not demand belief—it invites experience. It is less concerned with theology than with transformation. Its message is that enlightenment is possible, but it comes not through external authority, but through inner union. The divine spark is already within you. What remains is for you to remember it, nurture it, and allow it to guide you.

In a world that is often fragmented, distracted, and anxious, the voice of The Gospel of Philip is a healing sound. It calls us back to stillness, to intimacy, to the sacred. It invites us to see love not as weakness, but as the most powerful force in the universe—the force that creates, redeems, and transforms. Love is not a possession, but a presence. Not a transaction, but a revelation.

As you read this modern adaptation, let yourself enter the mystery it offers. Read slowly. Reflect deeply. Let the symbols speak to your own experience. Let the metaphors awaken memories of the soul. Let the gospel be not a book of doctrines, but a mirror in which you see the face of the divine in yourself. The truth is not far off. The Light is not hidden from those who seek it in love. The divine union is not reserved for the few—it is the inheritance of every soul that dares to remember where it came from and who it truly is.

This is not only the gospel of Philip. It is the gospel of wisdom, of reunion, of awakening. It is your gospel, too. Let it lead you to the inner chamber where love and truth meet, where division ends, and where the Light of the sacred burns in peace, clarity, and joy.

Gospel of Philip

A Hebrew welcomes another Hebrew into their community, calling them a "proselyte." However, while a proselyte can join the group, they cannot bring in another proselyte themselves. They remain as they are, shaped by those who accepted them, but they do not continue the cycle by bringing in others. Some people are creators and builders, while others simply exist without shaping or changing anything.

A slave longs for freedom, but even in their desire to be free, they do not expect to inherit their master's estate. A son, on the other hand, not only knows he is a son but also has a rightful claim to his father's inheritance. Those who inherit from what is dead are also bound to death, as they receive nothing but lifeless things. But those who inherit from what is truly alive gain both life and the inheritance of both the living and the dead. The dead cannot inherit anything, for how can something without life receive anything at all? Yet, if the dead were to inherit what is alive, they would no longer remain dead but would instead become fully alive.

A Gentile does not experience death in the same way as others because they were never truly alive to begin with. However, the one who believes in the truth has found real life. This new life also makes them vulnerable to death because only those who are alive can die. Since Christ came, the world has been changed—its cities transformed, and the dead brought out into the open. When we were Hebrews, we were like orphans, with only a mother to care for us. But when we became Christians, we gained both a father and a mother, becoming part of a divine family.

A person who plants seeds in winter will harvest their crops in summer. Winter represents this present world, while summer symbolizes the eternal realm. So, we should plant our seeds now in this life so we can reap the rewards of eternity. That is why we should not focus only on prayer in this world but also on what is to come. Just as summer follows winter, the eternal realm follows this temporary one. If someone tries to harvest in winter, they will not gather anything ripe—only unformed, useless crops. Just as barren land in winter cannot bring forth a full harvest, the Sabbath, without proper preparation, cannot bring life.

Christ came with a mission: to set some people free, to save others, and to redeem many. He ransomed those who were far from him, bringing them into his family. He saved those he had chosen, and he redeemed them according to his plan. His sacrifice did not begin at the moment of his arrival on earth; rather, he had been giving himself up willingly since the foundation of the world. When he came into the world, it was to reclaim what had already been his. That which belonged to him had fallen into the hands of thieves and been taken captive, but Christ came to rescue it. Through his sacrifice, he redeemed both the good and the evil in the world, leaving no one outside the reach of his grace.

Light and darkness, life and death, right and left—these opposites are connected, like siblings. They exist together, inseparable. Because of this, we must understand that good is not entirely good, nor is evil entirely evil. Life itself is not fully alive, and death is not completely dead. Everything will eventually return to where it came from. However, those who have risen above the contradictions of this world will not dissolve—they are eternal.

The words we use to describe things in this world can be misleading. They often take our thoughts in the wrong direction, distracting us from the truth. For example, when someone hears the word "God," they do not immediately grasp the full reality of who He is. Instead, they hold onto an imperfect idea. The same is true for words like "Father," "Son," "Holy Spirit," "life," "light," "resurrection," and "the Church." These words can be misunderstood unless someone truly understands the deeper meaning behind them. The names we use in this world are part of this world; they are not eternal. If they belonged to the eternal realm, they would not be expressed in the flawed language of this world. Eventually, these names will disappear when the eternal realm is fully revealed.

But there is one name that is not spoken in this world—the name that the Father gave to the Son. This name is greater than all names and fully expresses the Father's essence. The Son becomes one with the Father through this name. Those who have received it know it deeply, but they do not say it aloud. Those who have not received it remain unaware of its true power.

Truth gave names to things in the world so that we could understand them. Without names, learning would be impossible. Even though truth is one, it appears in many different forms so that we can recognize it. These names are used with love, helping us see how everything is connected to the same truth. However, the rulers of this world saw that humans were linked to what is truly good, and they wanted to deceive us. So, they took the names of what is good and attached them to things that were not good, hoping to confuse people and keep them under their control. But their trick ended up helping in an unexpected way. By creating lies, they forced people to search for what is real, making it easier to tell truth from falsehood and put everything in its rightful place.

The rulers of this world do not want humanity to be saved. They want to stay in power because if people find salvation, they will no longer need to offer sacrifices, which is what gives these rulers their strength. The animals placed on their altars were sacrifices meant for the rulers themselves—living creatures that were killed in the offering. But humanity was different. People were offered up in death, only to be given eternal life in return.

Before Christ came, the world did not have the true bread of life. It was like the Garden of Eden, where Adam lived. That garden had many trees that fed the animals, but it had no wheat to nourish human beings. In those times, people ate as animals did, without anything greater to lift them above their natural instincts. But when Christ arrived as the perfect human, he brought the true bread from heaven. This was not physical food, but spiritual nourishment, meant to feed the soul and help people rise above earthly things.

The rulers of the world believed they were acting on their own power, making choices freely. But in reality, the Holy Spirit was guiding everything, turning their actions into part of a greater divine plan. Truth, which has existed since the very beginning, is like a seed scattered throughout the world. Many people see it being planted, but only a few truly understand its purpose. The mystery of truth remains hidden from those who are not ready to receive it.

Some people have said, "Mary conceived by the Holy Spirit." But they misunderstand the deeper meaning of this mystery. When has a woman ever conceived a child through another woman? Mary is a pure and untouched virgin, undefiled by any power. Her role is a deep mystery and a challenge even to the Hebrews, including the apostles and their followers. She represents something beyond corruption, proving that the rulers of this world have no control over her. When Jesus spoke of "My Father who is in Heaven," he said it this way because he has another Father beyond the earthly one. If he had only meant an earthly father, he would have simply said, "My Father."

The Lord told his disciples, "Go out and gather people from every household, bringing them into the house of the Father. But take nothing from the house of the Father and do not carry anything away."

The name "Jesus" is mysterious and hidden, while "Christ" is a name that has been revealed. The name "Jesus" remains the same in every language, but "Christ" changes based on the language being spoken. In Syriac, it is "Messiah," and in Greek, it is "Christos." Every culture has its own way of saying it. "The Nazarene" is the one who makes hidden things visible. Christ contains everything—humanity, angels, mysteries, and even the Father himself.

Some people mistakenly say that the Lord died before he rose. But this is not true. He rose first and then died. To truly understand death, one must first experience resurrection. For as God lives, life comes before all things.

Think of it this way: No one hides a great treasure in a large, obvious place. Instead, valuable riches are often stored inside something small and ordinary. In the same way, the soul is a precious jewel, hidden within the human body, which may seem simple on the outside but holds something far greater within.

Many people are afraid of rising in the resurrection without a body, so they insist that they will rise in the flesh. But they don't understand that having flesh is actually a form of being naked. The ones who remove their earthly bodies are the ones who are truly clothed. "Flesh and blood cannot inherit the kingdom of God." What does this mean? It refers to our physical bodies, which are temporary. But what will enter the kingdom? Only what belongs to Jesus—his true flesh and blood. His flesh is the Word, and his blood is the Holy Spirit. Those who receive these will have eternal nourishment, drink, and clothing.

Some say that the flesh will not rise, while others insist that it will. Both are mistaken. To truly rise, one must go beyond the physical body, for everything already exists within it. In this world, people are more important than the clothes they wear. But in the kingdom of heaven, the garments of the soul are greater than the ones who wear them.

Everything is purified by water and fire. What we see is cleansed by visible things, and what is hidden is cleansed by invisible forces. Just as water exists within water, fire is present within the sacred anointing oil.

Jesus revealed himself to everyone in different ways, appearing in a form they could understand. To those who were great, he appeared as great. To those who were small, he appeared as small. To angels, he looked like an angel. To humans, he appeared as a man. Because of this, many did not truly recognize him; they only saw a reflection of themselves. But when he took his disciples up the mountain and revealed his true glory, he appeared in his full greatness, and they were made great enough to see him.

On that day, he gave thanks, saying, "You who have united the perfect light with the Holy Spirit, let the angels join us as reflections of that perfection."

Do not look down on the lamb, for it is the way to the king. No one can approach the king without it, and no one can enter his presence without being clothed.

The heavenly man has far more children than the earthly man. If the children of Adam are many, even though they die, how much greater are the children of the perfect man, who live forever. A father creates a son, but a son does not create another son; instead, he gains brothers. In this world, all are born in a natural way, but they are nourished by their true origin.

It is through the promise of heaven that humanity is sustained. The Word, which comes from that place, feeds the soul and leads it to perfection. The perfect ones give life through a kiss. That is why we greet one another with a kiss, sharing the grace that lives within us.

Three women always walked with the Lord: Mary, his mother; her sister; and Mary Magdalene, his companion. Each of them was called Mary, but each had a unique role in his life.

"The Father" and "the Son" are single names, but "the Holy Spirit" is a double name. It exists both above and below, in both what is seen and what is hidden. The Holy Spirit moves between both realms, connecting what is secret with what is revealed.

Without knowing it, the saints are sometimes served by evil powers. These powers are blinded by the Holy Spirit, making them think they are serving ordinary humans when they are actually serving the saints.

Once, a disciple asked the Lord for something of this world. The Lord replied, "Ask your mother, and she will give you what belongs to someone else."

The apostles said to the disciples, "May our offering be seasoned with salt so that it may be pleasing." They referred to wisdom as "salt," because without it, an offering would not be accepted. Wisdom does not bear children, and because of this, she is called "a trace of salt." But her barrenness does not mean she has no influence. Wherever she is present, the Holy Spirit moves, multiplying her children and making them many.

What the Father has also belongs to the Son. But as long as the Son is still a child, he is not given full authority over it. Only when he matures does the Father entrust him with everything, giving him his full inheritance.

Those who go astray or are led astray by the Spirit often fall because of that same Spirit. This is the mystery of its power: it can start a fire, and it can put one out, depending on its purpose.

Echamoth and Echmoth may sound similar, but they are not the same. Echamoth represents true wisdom—the divine knowledge that brings light and understanding. Echmoth, however, is the wisdom of death, tied to the knowledge of the physical world and everything that fades away. It is called "the little wisdom" because it belongs to things that do not last.

Think about the animals in the world. Some, like oxen and donkeys, live alongside people and help with work. Others are wild, roaming freely in deserts and forests. Farmers use domesticated animals to plow fields, and through their labor, both people and animals are fed. Even the wild animals benefit in some way from the land that is cultivated.

In the same way, the perfect man works in harmony with the forces that follow him, preparing everything for its purpose. Through this balance, everything in creation—both good and bad—exists together. The Holy Spirit watches over all things, guiding both the tame and the wild, ensuring that everything, even those who try to escape, remains within God's plan.

Creation reflects its source. Something that is created can be beautiful, but its offspring are not always noble. If something were begotten instead of made, its children would carry true nobility. But when something created gives birth, its offspring lack the full measure of divine greatness. This can be seen in the first acts of wrongdoing—adultery came first, and then from it, murder. The one born of adultery, the child of the serpent, became a murderer, taking his own brother's life. Every time two things that do not belong together are joined, it distorts the harmony of creation.

God is like a master dyer. Just as a cloth is dipped into dye and takes on its color, so God colors the soul with his eternal spirit. Those who are dyed in God's colors become immortal, for his colors never fade. He purifies his chosen ones, making them shine with his divine presence.

To truly see something, you must become like it. In the physical world, you can see the sun, the sky, the earth, and everything around you without becoming them. But in the higher realms, seeing and becoming are the same. When you see the Spirit, you become spirit. When you see Christ, you become like Christ. When you see the Father, you become one with him. In this vision, you are no longer separate; you merge with what you behold.

Faith is how we receive, and love is how we give. Without faith, a person cannot receive anything of true value. Without love, they cannot give in a way that matters. We believe so that we may receive, and we give out of love. Giving without love is empty—it is just an action without meaning. Those who receive anything apart from the Lord remain attached to the old ways, unable to rise above their earthly identity.

The apostles before us called him "Jesus the Nazorean, the Messiah," meaning "Jesus the Nazorean, the Christ." These names reveal who he is. "Jesus" in

Hebrew means "salvation." "Nazara" means "truth," and "the Nazarene" represents the very essence of truth. "Christ" means "the anointed one," signifying someone chosen and set apart for a divine purpose.

A pearl may be tossed into the mud and ignored, but its value does not change in the eyes of its owner. In the same way, the children of God always remain valuable, no matter where they are, for their Father always knows their worth.

If you call yourself a Jew, a Roman, a Greek, or a servant, no one will be disturbed. But if you say, "I am a Christian," the powers of the world will tremble. Just speaking this name unsettles the forces of darkness because it carries the authority of God.

God is like a "man-eater," receiving the sacrifices of humanity. Before people were offered as sacrifices, animals were given, because those who received them were not truly gods.

Both glass and clay pots are shaped by fire. If a glass vessel breaks, it can be melted down and reshaped, because it was formed through the breath of creation. But if a clay pot shatters, it is lost forever, because it lacks that same breath.

A donkey that walks in circles grinding grain may travel for miles, yet it never leaves the same spot. In the same way, some people work hard their entire lives but never move forward in what truly matters. At the end of all their efforts, they realize they have gained nothing—they have seen neither the works of man nor the wonders of God. Their labor has led them nowhere.

The eucharist represents Christ himself. In Syriac, he is called "Pharisatha," meaning "the one who is spread out," because he was stretched upon the cross to bring salvation to the world.

The Lord visited the dye works of Levi, where fabrics were colored using seventy-two different dyes. He took them all and placed them in a single vat. When he pulled them out, every fabric was pure white. He said, "Just as I have made all these colors one, the Son of Man has come to purify and unite all things."

Wisdom, often called barren, is the mother of angels. Mary Magdalene, who was close to Jesus, was loved by him more than the other disciples. He often kissed her on the lips, a sign of divine closeness. The disciples, seeing this, asked, "Why do you love her more than us?"

Jesus answered, "Why do you think I love her more than you? When a blind person and one who can see are in darkness, they are the same. But when the light comes, the one who sees will recognize it, while the blind will remain in darkness."

The Lord said, "Blessed is the one who existed before being born, for such a person is eternal and not bound by time. The eternal one has always been, is now, and always will be."

The greatness of a person is not something you can see with your eyes. It lies within. This hidden strength gives people mastery over animals, which may be physically stronger but lack understanding. Through wisdom, humans bring order to the wild. Without them, animals turn on each other, fighting and killing without purpose. It is man's labor—working the land and caring for the earth—that provides food and sustains life. Without this effort, nature remains in chaos.

If someone is baptized but does not receive the Holy Spirit, then calls themselves a Christian, they are only borrowing the name. They have taken on the title, but it comes with a responsibility they have not fulfilled. However, the one who truly receives the Holy Spirit does not borrow the name—it is given to them as a gift. A true gift requires no repayment, only acceptance. This is the difference between someone who has only claimed faith and someone who has truly been transformed by God's grace.

Marriage is a deep and sacred mystery. Without it, the world would not exist. The union of male and female continues life and reflects a divine truth. The existence of everything depends on this mystery, and within it lies great power. Yet, in the physical world, relationships are often flawed, and instead of reflecting divine unity, they sometimes reveal human weakness.

Evil spirits also take different forms—both male and female—seeking to corrupt what they can. Male spirits attach themselves to female souls, and female spirits attach themselves to male souls, taking advantage of those who are unguarded or disobedient. These spirits can only be overcome through divine power, which is given through the unity of the bridegroom and the bride, a symbol of the connection between God and the soul.

When lustful women see a man sitting alone, they approach him to lead him into temptation. In the same way, when corrupt men see a woman alone, they seek to take advantage of her. But when a man and woman are together in unity, neither male nor female spirits can harm them. This unity is a reflection of the sacred connection between the divine image and the angelic presence, which cannot be broken.

A person who rises above the world and no longer craves its temptations cannot be controlled by the forces that once held them back. They are beyond jealousy, fear, and temptation. But those who are still tied to the world remain vulnerable. If evil spirits come, they will take hold of a soul that does not have the Holy Spirit. Only those filled with the Spirit are safe, because no unclean force can touch them.

Do not be afraid of the body, but do not love it too much either. If you fear it, it will rule over you. If you love it too much, you will be trapped by it. The body is only a temporary covering, and being too attached to it keeps the soul from being free.

A person can be in one of three states: in the world, in resurrection, or stuck in between. No one should be caught in the middle! The world has both good and bad, but even the good in this world is not perfect, and the bad is not completely evil. However, the middle state—what some call death—is entirely empty and separated from God.

While we are alive, we should seek the resurrection. To enter resurrection means to prepare the soul for rest, to leave behind the body, and to rise above the state of being stuck between life and eternal light. Many people lose their way and become trapped in the middle, unable to move forward. It is better to leave this world in purity before sin takes hold, because the resurrection brings peace and unity with God. The middle place is a state of wandering, where the soul is neither fully in the world nor in the light.

We should strive to leave this world with grace, walking the path of righteousness. Then, when we leave our bodies behind, we can enter the eternal peace of resurrection instead of being lost in the middle. Those who walk this path overcome fear, sin, and death, finding unity with God forever.

Some people lack both the desire and the ability to do what is right. Others may have the will but do nothing. Neither is enough. In both cases, they fail because justice requires both desire and action together.

One of the apostles had a vision of people trapped in a burning house, bound by chains of fire. The flames surrounded them, and they cried out in pain and despair. Their faith had failed them. The apostle asked, "Why are you here? Can't you be saved?" They answered, "We never wanted to be saved. When salvation was offered, we ignored it. Now we suffer in the darkness because of our own choices."

The soul and spirit were created through water and fire, two of the essential elements of life. But the son of the bridal chamber was born through water, fire, and light. This fire is not destructive but pure and bright. It is the light that reveals all things.

Truth did not come into the world in its pure form because people were not ready to accept it. Instead, it was revealed through symbols and images. Even rebirth is hidden in imagery. To be reborn, a person must pass through the symbol of rebirth, which is resurrection. The image of resurrection must lead to the image of truth. The mysteries of the bridal chamber must also pass through these images before they can restore what was lost.

Those who speak of the Father, the Son, and the Holy Spirit must not just say the names but live by their truth. If they do not, even the title of "Christian" will be taken from them. One must receive the power of the cross, which the apostles described as "the right and the left."

A person who reaches this level is no longer just a follower of Christ—they become like Christ himself.

The Lord carried out everything with deep meaning: baptism, anointing, communion, salvation, and the sacred union. He said, "I came to make the things on earth reflect what is in heaven, to bring the outside and the inside together, and to create harmony in all things." His actions were filled with symbols and images, guiding people toward the full truth.

Some say, "There is a heavenly man, and another above him." This is incorrect. The first heavenly man, the one we see, is wrongly considered "lower," while the hidden one is thought to be "higher." A better way to describe it is "the inner, the outer, and what lies beyond the outer," because beyond the outermost darkness, nothing exists. The Lord called it "the outer darkness" because it is complete emptiness. He spoke of "My Father who is in secret" and taught, "Go into your room, close the door, and pray to your Father in secret," because the Father is present within all things.

Before Christ came, some people had left a place they could never return to, while others had entered a place they could never escape. Christ came to change this: he freed those who were trapped and brought home those who were lost.

When Eve stayed with Adam, there was no death. It was only when she separated from him that death began. If they reunite and become one again, death will come to an end.

On the cross, Christ cried out, "My God, my God, why have you abandoned me?" This marked the moment he left the earthly world to complete his divine mission.

A sacred union is not meant for animals, slaves, or those who are unclean. It is for those who are free and pure in spirit. Through the Holy Spirit, we are born again, and through Christ, we are anointed and made whole.

When we are reborn, we are joined together in the light and water of baptism. Light reveals truth, but it cannot be seen without something to reflect it, like a mirror or water. That is why baptism includes both light and water, with anointing as the light that cleanses and reveals.

In Jerusalem, three buildings were used for sacrifices. The western one was called "The Holy," the southern was "The Holy of the Holy," and the eastern was "The Holy of the Holies," which only the high priest could enter. Baptism is like "The Holy," resurrection is like "The Holy of the Holy," and the sacred union is like "The Holy of the Holies." The veil separating the sacred union was torn from top to bottom so that those below could rise up to the highest place.

The rulers of this world cannot see those who are clothed in perfect light, because the light protects them from harm. Those who are united in this light are free from the grasp of worldly powers.

If the woman had never been separated from the man, she would not have died. Separation was the beginning of death. Christ came to heal this division, bringing back together what was broken and restoring life to those who had been lost.

The union of man and woman in the sacred bond brings eternal unity, ensuring they will never be separated again. Eve was divided from Adam because she was joined to him outside this sacred bond. Christ came to restore this union in truth, offering eternal life to those who are united in it.

Adam's soul was given to him through God's breath, filling him with life. His true partner was the spirit, a divine gift meant to complete him. The earth, which was his mother, gave him a body to carry his soul. But later, his soul was replaced by the spirit, transforming him in ways that the rulers of the world could not understand. When Adam united with the spirit, he spoke words that went beyond human understanding. The rulers of the world became jealous because his connection to the spirit allowed him to understand mysteries they could not grasp. His spiritual partner was hidden from them, kept in a sacred space just for him—like a secret chamber that protected their union from corruption.

When Jesus arrived at the Jordan River, he brought with him the fullness of God's kingdom. He, who existed before all things, was born again. He, who had already been anointed, received a new anointing. He, who had been redeemed, became the one who would redeem others. His coming fulfilled a great divine mystery, bringing renewal to everything.

It is said that the Father of all united with a pure spirit that came down from above. On that day, a great light appeared, shining over the sacred place of divine union. From this, the body of Christ was formed—born from the holy bond between the bridegroom and the bride. Through this, Jesus established everything within the sacred union, a place of eternal peace and divine connection. Because of this, every disciple is called to enter that peace and take part in the unity that was destined from the beginning.

Adam was also created from two pure sources: the Spirit and the untouched earth. Christ, who was born of a virgin, came to undo the mistake that began with Adam's fall. He restored what was lost and repaired the separation between people and God.

In Paradise, there were two trees. One gave birth to animals, and the other gave birth to people. Adam, following his desires, ate from the tree that produced animals. By doing this, he became like them and passed on that nature to his children. Because of this, Adam's descendants began to worship animals, treating them as gods. But there was another tree—the one that created true people, made in God's image. This tree bore the fruit of life, but Adam never ate from it. This is similar to how people create their own gods and worship them, instead of realizing that it is the divine that should recognize humans as its creators.

A person's success depends on their abilities, and their achievements are the result of their hard work. One of their greatest achievements is their children, yet they are created not through struggle but through ease. This reflects a deeper truth: just as people work hard to build and create, their children are formed effortlessly.

This mystery mirrors something greater about the nature of the divine.

In this world, slaves serve the free, following the natural order of society. But in the Kingdom of Heaven, the free will serve the slaves. Those who have entered the sacred union—the children of the bridal chamber—will care for those still tied to the world. The children of the bridal chamber have only one purpose: rest. They do not need anything else because they exist in divine peace, beyond the need for change or transformation.

When someone enters the waters of baptism and rises again, their faith makes the water sacred. Baptism is not just a ritual—it is the fulfillment of righteousness, just as Jesus said: "This is how we fulfill all righteousness."

Some people believe they will die first and then rise again, but they are mistaken. If someone does not experience resurrection while they are alive, they will gain nothing after death. Baptism is not just about being cleansed—it is a great mystery of life. Those who receive it with faith gain eternal life, because baptism is a direct connection to resurrection.

The soul, spirit, and body are all connected in creation and salvation. Just as Adam's soul was later replaced by a spirit, each person must seek the divine unity that restores them to their true nature. Through baptism, resurrection, and the sacred union, people are given a path beyond the limits of this world, leading them into the eternal peace promised by Christ.

Philip the apostle once explained, "Joseph the carpenter planted a garden, needing wood for his work. From the trees he planted, he built the cross. And on that very cross, his own descendant hung. That descendant was Jesus, and the tree he planted became the cross itself." The Tree of Life stands at the center of the garden, but it was the olive tree that gave us the sacred oil. Through this oil, we receive resurrection and renewal, linking us to the divine.

This world consumes the dead, for it is a devourer of lifeless things. Everything it takes in eventually dies. But truth consumes what is living, and instead of death, it gives eternal nourishment. Those who are fed by truth will never die. Jesus came from this eternal place and brought divine food. To those who hungered for it, he gave life so they would never taste death.

God created a garden and placed man inside it. In this garden, choices had to be made, but there were also rules: "Eat this, but do not eat that." However, in the higher garden, where divine fulfillment exists, the rules are different. There, people freely eat from the Tree of Knowledge—not to bring death, but to receive life. In the lower garden, the Tree of Knowledge led to death.

The law, represented by that tree, taught people about good and evil, but it didn't lead them toward goodness or keep them from evil. Instead, it brought death because the command "Eat this, don't eat that" became the very thing that caused mankind to fall.

The sacred oil, known as chrism, is greater than baptism. We are called "Christians" because of the chrism, not baptism. The name "Christ" itself comes from this anointing. The Father anointed the Son, the Son anointed the apostles, and the apostles anointed us. Those who are anointed receive everything—resurrection, the light, the cross, and the Holy Spirit. These gifts are given in the sacred place of divine union. The Father and Son are united, with the Father in the Son and the Son in the Father. This is the Kingdom of Heaven, a place of unity and fulfillment.

Jesus spoke truthfully when he said, "Some entered the Kingdom of Heaven laughing, yet came out serious." Why? Because they rejected the world and its distractions, realizing how meaningless they were. When they entered the water, they left behind everything that tied them to the world and rose into something greater. If someone despises the world and sees it as unimportant, they come out of the water joyful, having received the peace of the Kingdom of Heaven. The same is true for the sacred bread, the cup, and the oil, though there is something even greater that awaits the faithful.

The world itself was created through a mistake. Its creator wanted to make it perfect and immortal but failed. Neither the world nor its maker will last forever. True eternal life belongs only to the children of God. Nothing can receive eternal life unless it first becomes a child of God, and one who does not have eternity within them cannot give it to others.

The cup of prayer holds wine and water, representing the blood of Christ for which people give thanks. This cup is filled with the Holy Spirit and belongs to those who have been made whole. Drinking from it allows people to receive the true life of Christ, taking on his essence. Before someone enters the water, they remove their old clothing, symbolizing the shedding of their mortal nature. Only then can they be clothed in the new life and receive eternity.

Just as a horse gives birth to horses and a man fathers children, a god brings forth gods. The bridegroom and the bride share this divine origin. They come from a sacred lineage that is not divided by the labels of this world. Before this origin, there was no Jew or Gentile—those who belong to the eternal realm are part of the true people, the children of the divine light.

In this world, relationships often have imbalance, with the husband's strength complementing the wife's perceived weakness. But in the eternal realm, these limitations do not exist. The unions there are greater than any in this world. They do not separate into different roles but exist as one, beyond the limits of flesh and mortality.

Those who have everything must know themselves. Without self-knowledge, they cannot truly enjoy their inheritance. But those who understand themselves will find joy and fulfillment in all they have because true understanding is the key to experiencing life in its fullest form.

The perfect person cannot be captured or even seen by the powers of this world. If they were seen, the powers would try to take hold of them, but they cannot grasp someone who is clothed in perfect light. To reach this state, a person must become light themselves, entering divine unity. Only then can they rise beyond the limitations of this world and leave behind the imperfection of the middle place, stepping fully into the eternal realm.

A priest is a sacred vessel, and everything he touches becomes holy. If he blesses the bread or the cup, how much more is his own body made holy, reflecting the divine presence within him?

Through baptism, Jesus removed death's hold. When we enter the waters, we no longer enter death—

we rise into new life. We are no longer trapped by the spirit of this world that brings the coldness of despair. Instead, when the Holy Spirit moves over us, it brings the warmth of renewal, filling us with the life of eternity.

The one who truly knows the truth is a free person. But this freedom is not shallow or worldly, because the free person does not live in sin. As it is written, "Anyone who sins is a slave to sin" (John 8:34). Truth is like a nurturing mother, and knowledge is like a guiding father. Together, they bring forth freedom and true understanding.

Some people believe that sin does not apply to them, and the world calls them "free." But this so-called freedom, based only on knowledge, often makes them proud. This is why it is said, "it makes them free." They feel above others, as if they have risen beyond the world. But knowledge alone is not enough. As it is written, "Love builds up" (1 Corinthians 8:1). True freedom does not come from knowledge alone but from knowledge combined with love.

Someone who is truly free, through deep understanding, chooses to serve others out of love—especially those who have not yet found freedom. Knowledge gives a person the ability to be free, but love connects them to others. Love does not separate or claim ownership, saying, "This belongs to me, and that belongs to you." Instead, love says, "Everything is yours."

Spiritual love is like the finest wine or the most fragrant oil. When a person is anointed with it, they feel joy and fulfillment. The fragrance of love benefits not only the one who carries it but also those around them. When a person filled with love is present, everyone nearby experiences its goodness. But if that person leaves, those who remain return to their original state, lacking that fragrance. This is like the Samaritan who poured wine and oil on the wounds of an injured man. The wine and oil were not just physical substances—they symbolized love and healing. As it is written, "Love covers a multitude of sins" (1 Peter 4:8).

The children a woman gives birth to often resemble the one who loves her. If her husband loves her, the children will look like him. But if she gives her heart to another man—someone who is not her husband—the children may carry his likeness instead. Even if she stays with her husband out of duty, her longing for someone else may influence the children she bears. In the same way, if you live with the Son of God, do not love the world, but love the Lord. If you do, the spiritual life you bring forth will reflect the Lord, not the broken image of the world.

In all creation, beings naturally connect with their own kind. Humans gather with humans, horses stay with horses, and so on. This reflects a deeper truth: spirit joins with spirit, thought connects with thought, and light unites with light. If you remain human in nature, people will embrace you. But if you rise to a higher level and become spirit, then spirit will unite with you. If you become pure thought, thought will blend with you. If you become light, light will shine within you. Those who belong to the divine realm will rest upon you if you align yourself with them.

But if you lower yourself to the level of an animal—acting like a horse, a donkey, a bull, or a dog—then neither humanity, spirit, thought, nor light will connect with you. Neither those from above nor those from within will recognize or rest in you. In this state, you will have no part in what is divine or eternal.

A slave who is forced into servitude may one day be freed. But someone who was set free by their master's kindness and then willingly returns to slavery may never be freed again. This is the great loss of someone who turns away from the freedom they were given.

Farming in the natural world requires balance among four key elements: water, earth, wind, and light. Only when these elements work together can the harvest be gathered into the barn. In the same way,

God's spiritual work depends on four things: faith, hope, love, and knowledge. Faith is like the earth, providing the foundation where we grow. Hope is like water, sustaining and strengthening us. Love is like the wind, helping us grow and expand. Knowledge is like the light, guiding us toward full maturity.

Grace is shown in four ways: it comes from the earth, descends from heaven, reaches the highest places, and extends beyond what we can understand. These forces work together, just like the elements of nature support life.

Through these mysteries, we learn that knowledge alone cannot bring true freedom without love. Real freedom doesn't come from pride in what we know but from humility in serving others and connecting with the divine. Love moves like the wind, and knowledge shines like light, helping the soul grow until it is ready to take its place in eternity.

Blessed is the person who has never caused harm or suffering to another soul. Such a person is truly like Christ. Jesus himself lived this way—he brought light and comfort without adding burdens to anyone. He was the perfect man, but perfection is difficult for us to define. How can we, who are imperfect, reach such greatness? How can we bring comfort to everyone, no matter who they are, without causing pain to anyone?

It is not right to hurt someone and then only comfort those who deserve it. Some find it easy to bring comfort to those who are already at peace, but truly good people do not choose whom they help based on personal desires. Sometimes, even when a righteous person does not intend to cause harm, others may still feel troubled by their presence. This is often because the good person's actions reveal the flaws in others, making them uncomfortable.

Think of a man who owns a large estate filled with everything: children, servants, cattle, dogs, pigs, wheat, barley, hay, grass, and even acorns and meat. Because he is wise, he knows what to give each one. He gives bread to his children, simple food to his servants, barley and grass to the cattle, bones to the dogs, and acorns and slop to the pigs.

A true follower of God is like this man. He understands each person's soul and gives them what they need to grow. He does not judge people by their outward appearance but looks deeper into their spirit. To those who are like pigs, he gives what suits them. To those like cattle, he gives what they need. To those like children, he shares the fullness of divine wisdom.

There is the Son of Man, and there is the son of the Son of Man. The Lord is the Son of Man, and the son of the Son of Man is one who creates through the authority of the Son. The Son of Man was given the power to create and give life by God. Creating and giving life are two different things. A creator works in a way that everyone can see, while the one who gives life does so in a hidden way, unseen by the world. This hidden process is a deep mystery of divine unity.

Marriage in this world is a mystery, even to those who are part of it. No one truly knows the bond between a husband and wife except the two of them. If a physical marriage is already such a mystery, how much greater is the mystery of a spiritual marriage? This sacred union is pure, born from love, not physical desire. It belongs to the light, not the darkness. If a marriage becomes public, it loses its holiness and becomes ordinary. A bride should reveal herself only to those closest to her—her parents, the friend of the bridegroom, and the sons of the bridegroom. Others may only hear her voice or experience her presence from a distance, like dogs waiting for crumbs at their master's table.

When Abraham received a vision of what was to come, he circumcised himself as a sign of removing his earthly nature. In the same way, spiritual truths are hidden inside us, giving life, but if they are revealed too soon, they can bring harm instead.

As long as a tree's roots are hidden, it can grow strong. But if its roots are exposed, the tree will wither and die. The same is true for evil—when it remains hidden, it continues to grow in power. But once it is recognized and brought into the light, it disappears. This is why the Word says, "The axe is already at the root of the trees" (Matthew 3:10). The axe does not just cut the surface, because anything cut can grow back. Instead, it strikes deep, destroying evil at its source.

Jesus came to remove the root of evil completely, while others have only scratched the surface. We must also search within ourselves and remove any evil that remains. If we ignore it, it will continue to grow and control us, making us do things against our will. Ignorance is the source of all evil, keeping people trapped in sin and death.

Ignorance leads to death because those who live in ignorance have no foundation in truth. They never truly existed in the way that matters. They were, are, and will be nothing because ignorance produces nothing lasting. Truth, however, may seem hidden like ignorance at first, but when it is revealed, it brings life and is praised. As the Word says, "If you know the truth, the truth will set you free" (John 8:32). Ignorance enslaves, but knowledge brings freedom.

When we embrace the truth, we will see its fruits grow within us. By joining ourselves with truth, we are made whole, for knowing and accepting the truth is the key to freedom and eternal life. We must remove ignorance and cultivate truth, allowing it to transform us into beings of light and freedom.

Right now, we see the world as it appears on the surface. People are taught to admire the strong and powerful, while those who seem weak or unimportant are ignored. But in the divine realm, things are the opposite. What the world sees as weak is actually strong, and what is overlooked holds great value in the hidden truth. Though the mysteries of truth are revealed to us, they come in symbols and images, giving us only a glimpse of something far greater than we can fully understand.

The bridal chamber is the most sacred and profound of all mysteries. It is the most holy place, hidden from view. In the past, a veil covered the way God controlled creation, keeping divine truths secret. But when the veil was torn, those mysteries were revealed. When this world's time is over, it will no longer stand—it will be abandoned and eventually destroyed. The lesser powers that once ruled over it will flee, but they cannot enter the place of pure and perfect light, where the fullness of the divine exists. Instead, they will remain under the shadow of the cross, unable to reach the highest truth.

Those who are part of the divine priesthood will find safety when the flood of destruction comes. They will pass through the torn veil, just as the high priest once did, and enter the sacred space. The veil was not only torn from the top, which would have opened the way only for the heavens, nor from the bottom, which would have only revealed it to the earth. Instead, it was torn from top to bottom, opening a path from heaven to earth. The higher realms have revealed the mysteries of the lower realms so that we may understand divine truth.

This opening reveals a power and glory far greater than anything in this world. The perfection of the divine realm, along with its hidden mysteries, has now been made known to us. The holiest place has been revealed, and the bridal chamber welcomes those who wish to enter.

As long as evil remains hidden, it has no power. But it still exists among those who carry the Holy Spirit, controlling many people without them realizing it. When evil is exposed and brought into the light, the perfect light will shine over everything. Those who remain in this light will receive the anointing that sets them free. The enslaved will be freed, and those held captive will be released. As it is written, "Every plant my

Father in heaven has not planted will be pulled up" (Matthew 15:13).

Those who were once separated from God will be reunited with Him and filled with His light. Everyone who enters the bridal chamber will carry this light, showing their eternal union with the divine. Unlike earthly marriages, which happen at night and fade away with the morning, the sacred marriage of the soul and the divine takes place in the light of day and lasts forever. This light never sets and never fades.

To become a child of the bridal chamber is to receive this eternal light. But if someone does not receive it in this life, they will not be able to receive it in the next. Those who receive the light of the bridal chamber become invisible to the powers of this world. They cannot be captured, harmed, or controlled, even while living in this world. And when they leave this world, they will already be filled with truth because they have encountered it through these mysteries.

For those who enter the bridal chamber, this world is transformed into something eternal, and they experience the divine realm in its fullness. To them, the truth is no longer hidden in darkness but is revealed in perfect light. This light never ends and shines on all who are united with it, guiding them toward the greatest mysteries of the divine.

Translated by Tim Zengerink

The path to the bridal chamber is both an invitation and a discovery. It calls us to go beyond what we see in this world, to embrace the hidden truth, and to step into the eternal light where we are no longer held back by darkness and ignorance.

Thank You for Reading

Dear Reader,

We hope this timeless classic has sparked your imagination and enriched your literary journey. Now that you've turned the final page, we want to share a vision for the future of reading—one where every classic you've ever wanted to explore is at your fingertips, in a format that best suits your life.

We'd like to invite you to gain immediate, unlimited digital & audiobook access to hundreds of the most treasured literary classics ever written—along with the option to secure deluxe paperback, hardcover & box set editions at printing cost. Together, we can spark a new global literary renaissance alongside our small, independent publishing house called "The Library of Alexandria."

Thousands of years ago, the Library of Alexandria stood as a beacon of knowledge—until it was lost to history. We aim to reignite that spirit of preservation and discovery right now, in the modern age—only this time, it's accessible to all, in every language and every format.

Picture a world where every timeless classic, novel, poem, or philosophical treatise is not only available to read but also updated for today's readers—modernized, translated into any language or dialect, and ready to enjoy in any format you choose, whether that is in an eBook, audiobook, paperback, or deluxe hardcover & box set version a printing cost.

By joining our movement to rebuild the modern Library of Alexandria, you become part of an unprecedented mission to offer:

- **Unlimited Audiobook & eBook Access to the Greatest Classics of All Time**

    Instantly explore thousands of legendary works, from Plato and Shakespeare to Jane Austen and Leo Tolstoy. All are instantly ready to read or listen to, giving you a complete literary universe at your fingertips.

- **Paperback & Deluxe Editions at Printing Costs:**

    Purchase any title in a paperback, deluxe hardbound, or deluxe boxset edition at printing costs, shipped right to your doorstep. Curate your personal library of Alexandria with editions worthy of display—crafted to last, designed to captivate, and delivered straight to your door.

- **Modern translations for Contemporary Readers in all languages and dialects**

  Discover a vast selection of classics reimagined in clear, current language—no more struggling with outdated phrases or obscure references. Next to the original versions, we aim to offer translations in as many languages and dialects as possible.

  As we continue our translation efforts and add new languages, readers everywhere can connect with these works as if they were written today. By bridging linguistic divides, you're contributing to ensuring that these timeless stories become more meaningful, accessible, and inspiring for people across the globe.

- **Your Personal Library of Alexandria:**

  Over the months and years, you'll curate a unique physical archive of classics—each volume a testament to your taste, curiosity, and love of knowledge. It's not just about owning books—it's about curating a cultural legacy you'll cherish and pass down for generations to come.

- **Join a Global Literary Renaissance:**

  Your support fuels an ongoing mission: allowing us to reinvest in offering deluxe print editions (including special boxsets) at their true cost, broaden the range of available formats and translations, and extend the reach of these works to new audiences worldwide. By joining today, you're not just preserving a legacy of masterpieces; you set in motion a powerful wave of literary accessibility.

We are more than a publisher—we're a movement, and we can't do it alone. Your support lets us scale our mission, preserving and reimagining history's greatest works for tomorrow's readers.

Become a Torchbearer of knowledge.

Thank you for picking up this book and allowing us into your literary journey. As you turn the pages, know that you're part of something larger: a global effort to keep these stories alive, share their wisdom across borders and generations, and spark a true cultural revival for the modern era.

If this resonates with you—please consider taking the next step by visiting:

www.libraryofalexandria.com

With gratitude and a shared love of knowledge,

The Modern Library of Alexandria Team

Visit:

www.libraryofalexandria.com

Or scan the code below:

www.ingramcontent.com/pod-product-compliance
Lightning Source LLC
LaVergne TN
LVHW030631080426
835512LV00021B/3456